Warm Dogs in Heaven

Kevin Rottweiler

PublishAmerica
Baltimore

First printing

PublishAmerica has allowed this work to remain exactly as the author intended, verbatim, without editorial input.

Hardcover 978-1-4560-3072-8
Softcover 978-1-4560-3073-5
PUBLISHED BY PUBLISHAMERICA, LLLP
www.publishamerica.com
Baltimore

Printed in the United States of America

Dogs in Heaven

Warm dogs in Heaven,
Moist snout excitement.

Paws cuddle the rested,
Release burdens' confinement.

In Heaven the dogs don't bite,
Pink tongues and lips are tested.

Herding sheep is what they do,
Working class dogs amused.

Relaxing on brilliant rainbows,
Pit Bull clamping all defused.

Lightening never threatens,
Dogs wearing golden crowns.

There will be warm dogs above,
Sea of glass surely surrounds.

Singing in the Barn

I can't believe, I hear the dogs singing in the barn,
All in perfect alignment, such a wonderful
assignment.

One by one, they sing out loud, nature's sweet alarm;
Tails swinging merrily, paws held up in such delight!

And they know the songs of old, Basset Hound and a
trumpet sound;
"How Great Thou Art" they hymn, including
"Amazing Grace."

German Shepherds, Labradors and Rottweilers have
found,
That singing in the barn, takes them closer to
Heaven's gates.

Now the cold rain pours down, but there is no time to
fret.
Moist, dampened fur, with a mildew smell and fleas!

God is watching over these dogs and puppies, you bet;
The altar is open immediately, and all the dogs are on
their knees.

Hospice Dogs

When the end is near,
I refuse to shed a tear.

Warm dogs surround my bed,
My soul I voluntarily shed.

Hot kisses and days-gone-bye,
Moist snouts and kennel flies.

Like angels, they surround me,
Quieting life's chronology.

Beagles, Hounds and Labradors,
Prepare me for Heaven's shores.

Golden Arches

Sweet Dakota,
Your cancer spread.

A form of Lymphoma,
Is all they said.

They drove you,
To the Golden Arches.

I learned to love you,
Winter snow through March.

The yellow wrapper,
And your tasty tongue.

Cheeseburger into your snapper,
Freedom has just begun.

Now you soar,
By the Golden Arches.

Life eternal and evermore,
Watching you by the herbal marshes.

You must be home Dakota,
God just called your name.

Dog Boat

On the port side, the waves had died down,
Now the sky turned an eerie apple green;
Basset Hound made the trumpet sound.

Noah nervously counted the dogs,
Even the tape worms felt uneasy;
The horizon reeked of a murky-sulfur fog.

Dogs vomited their early biscuits,
Motion sickness stole their confidence;
The smell of burning rubber and smoldering crickets.

Day pirates ate insects from the wood planks,
Noah kept track of the ruminants;
Cow sores and glands, seeking drainage in the sand.

The small fires on board, kept creatures warm,
Hobos and drifters sucked rum from dirty bottles;
Squirrels, mice, rats and crabs swarmed.

Paranoid dogs peek through port holes,
Reassurance is hard to come by,
Dogs below the oily deck, living like moles.

An Irish Setter found a ball to play with,
Other dogs just kept their territory personal;
Icy hurricane rain only feeding satan's bliss.

Dogs, dogs, peeking through dirty port holes,
Whining and crying with muffled sounds;
Dogs, dogs, peeking through algae port holes.

Something tall and erect, with the stature of a King, or a man,
Just walked on the surface of the water, the dogs turned white;
From this day on, chronology has a plan…
Now the sea is calm.

Dog Pound

Yelps
Barks
Moans
Whispers

Loneliness
Darkness
Quiet
Depression

Heartbeats
Warmth
Paws
Snouts

Coolness
Breathing
Moist
Snouts

Water
Pooper scooper
Shoes
Pails

Injection
Music
Euthanasia
Heaven

Growling
Aggression
Confession
Quiet

Reflections
Shiny
Aluminum
Cages

Sponges
Cleaning
Bleach
Pails
Visitors
Smiles
Hope
Love

Biscuits
Sun
Moon
Day break

Visitors
Vaccinations
Adoption
Home

Oh Starr

Pit Bull, Oh pitiful,
Leader of alpha confusion.

Plentiful in spirit, plentiful,
But you lack sweet fusion.

Dog without a home,
Waiting for a family.

A little space to roam,
Sometimes you are jolly.

But you fought me,
And tried to take the leash.

Growling, growling, she…
I shook like a leaf.

With full capacity to maul,
Nobody took you serious.

Are you in for the long haul?
Cage aggression and desperation?

But Starr,
You finally made it!

Found a family from afar,
Tug-of-war and dog biscuits.

The Meal

Oh hungry Mastiff,
Salivate and wiggle.
Chunks of meat,
And maybe a pickle.

You waited quietly,
For the main course.
Bow your head shyly,
The size of a horse.

This dinner only says,
How we care for you, “miracle girl.”
Holding off till the next day,
Neopolitan Mastiff; blue swirl.

Folds of flesh and pockets of love,
Strong bones mesh together.
You must have seen a dove,
Now begin sunny weather.

We fill your stomach to the gills,
And YOU protect us at night.
Paying all the veterinary bills,
Sweet Mastiff, worth the fight.

Nora the Shepherd

Sweet Nora,
Studies the Bible at night.

Sweet Nora,
A wonderful sight.

Sweet Nora,
German Shepherd mix.

Sweet Nora,
Praying near candlesticks.

Sweet Nora,
Will go to Heaven.

Sweet Nora,
Lamp stand's golden seven.

Dog Stones

Bright stones boast of color,
Amethyst, Jasper and Topaz.

Blue sky; confident cheerful summer,
A place where eternal life lasts.

Large, junk yard dogs, running;
Through the dung gate and horse gate.

Meaty dogs, wander in New Jerusalem,
Fed by city dwellers from Heaven.

Sniffing the shiny stones,
Large dogs tenderly roam.

Shaded by palm trees,
Taking refuge under Myrtle trees.

Bright stones boast of color,
Onyx, Agate and Sapphire.

Pink sky; warm lemonade summer,
The face of Jesus Christ always lasts.

Large, junk yard dogs, yawning,
Through the sheep gate and fish gate.

Dog Prayer Number One

God in Heaven:
Thank you for this day.
Thanks for creating my paws, my snout and my tail.

God I thank you:
For allowing me to serve my master,
Your friend.

I enjoy your wonderful trees,
Green grasses and flower beds, Lord.
I enjoy drinking from crystal fountains.

God above:
Thank you for this day.
My little dog house keeps out the rain.

I receive food and water from my master,
I vigorously protect my human family,
Thanks for giving me a purpose, Lord.

God in Heaven:
Thanks for helping my master find a job,
My human family feeds me and cuddles me,
I would be at the pound if they did not exist.

God I thank you:
For allowing me to walk the earth,
I am so afraid of the animal control division.

Please comfort me in your arms Lord,
When that day comes, and they cart me away.
I don't want to die at a lonely kennel.

The sound of crying and moaning barks,
Only brings your love closer to me,
Please don't let them hurt me.

And if I die there Lord,
I will try and be courageous;
Prepare me for Heaven's shores.

Dog Prayer Number Two

Lord, thank you for this day,
You comforted me at the animal hospital,
Your loving-kindness astounds my master.

I once prayed to you from the car,
I know you heard my cries and barks,
Your sweetness is candy for my soul.

Lord, thank you for this day,
I will keep my mouth shut,
Never, never, will I bite a child.

Keep me strong in your arms, Lord,
You comforted me when my puppies were born,
I licked and kissed their warm snouts.

Lord, you understand my needs,
I understand they are waiting for me in Heaven, when that day comes;
You are my Father that engulfs me.

When I got hit by the car, Lord,
I called your name,
My golden crown was prepared.

Now as I get older,
I need your special touch on my fur;
Your love is more than enough.

Someday, I will see your robes,
You are the Great Veterinarian,
In which my love to you secretly unfolds.

I wag my tail for all the children, and for the old people.
I hope they know who constructed me,
You are the Son of God that warms me.

At Church

What a wonderful sight!
Dogs coming in, and tails wagging merrily,
Up the aisle they go, without a fight.

Stained glass windows, allows God to shine;
Dogs sitting in the pews, waiting so happily.
At church they never bark, they never whine.

Poodles and Golden Doodles,
Dachshunds,
Rottweilers
Shepherds,
Basset Hounds
Labs,
and
Sheepdogs.

After church, a taste for spaghetti and noodles.

Baptism Dogs

The groomer's tub was full of water,
Now Rufus gathered up all the dogs,
Some said prayers, as others trembled.

Rufus the Rottweiler took control,
Pushing and shoving each dog, into the water.
Lining up, with an Alpha Roll—sins are forgiven!

Rex the Pit Bull declared, "Baptism in the name of Jesus."
All kinds of dogs, waited patiently in line,
A Bulldog danced a soft shoe Jitterbug.

Rufus the Rottweiler took control,
Now displaying love and affection, sparingly;
A place for counseling, confession and baring souls,
Church talk and socializing, part of the show.

Again, lining up, dozens of warm dogs,
Vigorously leaping by faith, into the cold spiritual bath.
Tails wagging, canine grins, sins are all gone!

Heaven

LOVE
LOVE
LOVE
LOVE LOVE LOVE LOVE
LOVE
LOVE
LOVE
LOVE
LOVE
LOVE
LOVE
LOVE
LOVE
LOVE

(John 3:16)

Bad Dogs

Breaking into the pantry was no big deal,
Dogs hungry and thirsty after church.

Now this was not an ordinary meal,
The pastor was gone as the devil lurked.

Craziness in their eyes,
Excited paws broke into the wine cabinet.

Now the church didn't keep wine,
However, some grape juice from the 1900s spoiled over time.

Big meaty dogs, poured the fermented juice down hot pink throats,
Bad dogs, bad dogs they are.

A poodle yelped and did the Polish Polka,
A German Shepherd danced like John Travolta.

One dog admitted her sins and recited English folklore,
Others flashed photographs with a Minolta.

One by one the dogs swallowed and gulped the fermented grape juice,
Dancing and laughing, getting loose.

A game of cards and gambling began in the back room,
Poker chips were dealt out by the Pit Bulls.

A Rottweiler ordered several pizzas, others wanted breadsticks,
The Basset Hounds argued about who was going to the moon.

A male Schnauzer spun one of the bottles on the floor, laughing;
Some of the female dogs were disgusted.

The dogs ripped up the pantry, chewing all the cupboards,
Smashing cookie jars and bread loafs torn.

Drunken Labradors competed for sardines,
Fish oils, sugar, flour, coffee grounds, maple syrup on the floor!

Poodles, Hounds, Sheepdogs and Bullmastiffs partied; they boogied.
The midnight janitor, thirsty for coffee…opened the door.

Pit Bull Ownership

Talk to loyal Pit Bull owners

Talk to animal control officers

Talk to Pit Bull breeders

Talk to dog trainers

Talk to dog behaviorists

Talk to animal shelter workers

Talk to your neighbors

Talk to kennel owners

Talk to veterinarians

Talk to dog groomers

Talk to veterinary technicians

Talk to veterinary assistants

Talk to kennel volunteers

Talk to dog adoption counselors

Talk to paramedics

Talk to attorneys

Talk to emergency room physicians

Talk to your children

Talk to God

Talk to your spouse

Talk to your family

Talk to your new Pit Bull

Dirty Babylon

Seventy or more years strong,
Nebuchadnezzar was all wrong.
Wolves and jackals mournfully cried,
A sinful city where people died.

Altars, hanging gardens and temples,
Many have defiled God's laws.
Buried clay tablets of 10 B.C.,
Why aren't these people free?

Dirty city of painful greed,
Purposefully planting all the wrong seeds.
Struggles, civil unrest, falls and wars,
Losing gold from its very own stores.

People must tear down these walls,
As helpless souls; sucked into waterfalls.
Let's now go forward with God's grace,
Admit the strength, in Jesus face.

Sled Dogs

Oh freight dogs of the north,
Alaskan Malamutes, Eskimo dogs and Siberian
Huskies;
We're going to Heaven, to praise the Lord.

Hauling food, supplies and medicine,
Wonderful snow dogs very industrious;
Carried diphtheria serum through an epidemic.

Kissing the sled master on the chin,
Tough as nails, with wintery coats;
In Heaven, snow dogs truly win.

Some jumped off their team to shovel,
Never are they very short-handed;
It is God's heart they have landed.

Piling snow around the throne,
Solid work ethic and trustworthy;
Honest eyes just searching for soup bones.

A Dog's House Rules

1. You shall honor your master
2. You shall love your neighbor
3. You shall love God
4. You shall not kill
5. You will never bite a human
6. You will never bite a child
7. You shall honor your mother and father
8. You will never steal dog biscuits
9. You shall attend dog obedience classes
10. You shall attend church

Street Dogs

The streets of Jerusalem sweet,
Crowded cobblestone paths and moist stones,
A royal city of prophets and Jesus.

But the dogs are out,
Peering over the Dome of the Rock;
Fierce-looking street dogs, with tough snouts.

They wander in packs, licking their lips,
So hungry for meat,
Constant searching, walking and day trips.

The smell of bread and fresh fish,
A Jewish boy throws meat to the dogs,
A morsel, a tidbit, for hungry, hungry lips.

The old Herodian Wall attempts to contain the dogs,
As observant dogs gallop to the Fish Gate;
Men of Tyre, sell their wares and fish here.

Paradise the Cocker Spaniel

Pink tongues, licking vanilla ice cream cones,
Sweet natured Cocker Spaniels;
Like show dogs, confident, with a merry disposition.

A bird dog, retrieves coconut rainbows,
Kisses so sweet, makes the heart beat.
A natural dancer and prancer, there she goes.

Paradise is a puff of fresh spearmint air,
She enjoys brooks of honey and butter;
A dog that will cling to Heaven's golden stairs.

No more doggie bags, no more fleas,
No more vaccinations; pain and suffering gone.
In Paradise, no more waves, no stormy seas.

Pink tongues, kissing the royal gates,
A sweet gel drips from Aloe branches;
To Heaven, Cocker Spaniels are never late.

Paradise is a sunny day lasting forever,
Blue and pink sky sunsets,
Dog tails wag, so merrily on Heaven's shores.

Pet Cemetery

Over on Burdick Street is a pet cemetery,
I walked so many dogs by there,
Not far from the cattery.

You see people crying from their car
windows,
Hugging and hugging and struggling,
Rain comes down so humid and cold.

But they have forgotten Heaven's shores,
Weak faith and without Jesus Christ,
Life has become stale and boring.

Over on Burdick Street is a pet cemetery,
I walked so many dogs by there,
Not far from the cattery.

Mouthy Doggies

Mouthy doggies,
Chewing on twigs,
Mouthy doggies,
Biting at figs.

Mouthy doggies,
Chewing at Aloe,
Mouthy doggies,
Biting at Mallows.

Mouthy doggies,
Chewing at weeds,
Mouthy doggies,
Biting at trees.

Mouthy doggies,
Chewing at vines,
Mouthy doggies,
Gulping wine.

Dog Angels

The Bloodhound finds lost children,

The German Shepherd guides the blind,

Bullmastiffs guard property and estates,

Toy dogs, comforting and kind.

Dog Poet

Eccentric

Electric

Funny

Humor

Gloom

Rumor

Doom

Pens

Paper

Dog Shores

A blue sky above, lasting forever,
Starfish and barnacles, sand pebbles;
A Labrador yawns, perfect display of sunny weather.

Waves cool my feet, ripples and tides,
The dog smiles with contentment;
In Heaven, an honest soul never dies.

Shiny rocks, granite and agate,
Little creatures, fish and seagulls;
Labrador barks, eating from a full plate.

A charcoal fire, the cooking of bread and fish,
Nets overflowing, an honest catch;
Well-known disciples with multitudes of fish.

Jesus smiled as onlookers observed,
Now the Labrador took a nap;
A blue sky above, lasting forever.

Pooch

What a nice warm creature,
Sits at my feet,
Is nature's teacher.

And we go walking,
Pooch pretends to listen,
I do all the talking.

Pooch is a large senior Hound,
Seeking a family home,
Isn't the type found at the pound.

I rubbed Pooch's belly,
For half an hour,
Fatty layers, shook like jelly.

Pooch looked up in ecstasy,
Like a party, friends everywhere,
What a holiday!

What a nice warm creature,
Sits at my feet,
Is nature's teacher.

Dog Ladder

The most muscular dogs were summoned,
Fierce-looking, powerful and strong.
Like soldiers at a gate, they held up the ladder,
Dogs, one-by-one; some were sad, some had laughter.

Up- up- and-away, dogs walking, up to Heaven,
An honest climb; but sin knows no season.
A mile high it seemed,
Hearts a pumping, dog breath clean.

Dog faces, expressions, and confusion,
Dog faces, expecting, and questioning.
Tails wagging, with a cheerful display of love,
Up the ladder, dozens, just a push-and-shove.

In harmony, dogs, leaving the ground,
Nobody made a barking sound.
Such cooperation, a smooth operation,
In synchrony, dogs up to Heaven.

Water From Rocks

In the wilderness, it was frightening,
Lacking resources and the water supply tightening.

So Moses talked to God about it;
The solution was to extract water, from rocks split.

Shepherds gathered around the dogs,
Gaining their trust, and talked about rocks.

Immediately the muscular animals went to work,
Pulling massive stones from earth, a symbolic new birth.

Pit Bulls, Rottweilers and Mastiffs cracked,
Gigantic stones rolled off their backs.

Granite boulders,
As high as their shoulders.

Now striking the pointed stones,
Rewarding the dogs, with beefy soup bones.

Water emerged in a stream,
Blood of life, cookies and cream.

Clean Water

Water scarce in Palestine,
Goatskins swelled with the precious fluid;
People competing for this clear wine.

Ceremonial washing and the Water of Bitterness,
Remove this impurity and take away sin;
Water for cleanliness.

Water of Jealousy, please refresh our souls,
Punish those who are guilty;
Water carried in earthen jars and bowls.

Oh sweet Baptism, can you save us?
Lie me down in that cold watery grave,
Purify our souls Lord; Water of Separation.

A waterspout could redeem Babylon,
Oral cavities, tongues so parched and dry;
The only way to peace is through the Son.

Water scarce in Palestine,
Goatskins swell with the precious fluid;
People compete for this clear wine.

Sun Stood Still

During the battle of Gibeon,
The dogs were howling.
And with Joshua's victory,
Left the dogs a growling.

The sun stood still,
Everything was out of whack.
Pertaining to this city-hill,
God was covering Joshua's back.

Even the moon stopped,
Nature so confused,
Dogs with tails newly cropped,
Puppies yawning, so amused.

Now Labradors stepped out,
Hoping for an hour long tan,
Basset Hound made the trumpet sound,
Such an awesome miracle, outside of Heaven.

The Valley of Aijalon,
Where dogs often strayed;
As the moon called to them,
Innocent dog bones lay.

Job

In the Land of Uz,
So much suffering,
But Job loved God.

The devil was on his back,
Job lost everything,
His family was under attack.

But dogs came into Job's life,
Licked his sores clean,
Threw away problems; strife.

A Labrador became Job's friend,
Gave him friendship,
Unconditional love to lend.

Job loved God,
He did not sin,
The dogs helped him win.

That Lab,
Chased away the devil,
Job's depression and heartache lifted.

Noah Knows God

Noah, a tender man, knows Jesus;
Carries about his usual business.
Up in Heaven, cleaning the kennel cages,
Helping each dog, through its life stages.

Has given his soul, to God's very grace,
Noah has seen God's Holy face;
He put the animals into the ark,
Pairs of innocent dogs that bark.

Noah, is only doing what's right,
Courageously met the devil with fight.
Please follow these men of rapture,
Sowing seeds of mankind's capture.

Daily toil, sweats from his brow,
Noah checks upon the cows;
Always wanted to be a veterinarian,
But he cared for animals in the great millennium.

Noah, an honest man knows God,
As the brilliant rainbow displays.
Each and every shelter dog,
Has peace and joy with God's grace.

Heaven Bound Dogs

American Water Spaniel
Brittany Spaniel
Chesapeake Bay Retriever
Clumber Spaniel
Cocker Spaniel
Curly-Coated Retriever
English Cocker Spaniel
English Setter
English Springer Spaniel
Field Spaniel
Flat-Coated Retriever
German Shorthaired Pointer
German Wirehaired Pointer
Golden Retriever
Gordon Setter
Irish Setter
Irish Water Spaniel
Labrador Retriever
Pointer
Sussex Spaniel
Vizsla
Weimaraner
Welsh Springer Spaniel
Wirehaired Pointing Griffon
Afghan Hound
American Foxhound
Basenji
Basset Hound
Beagle
Black & Tan Coonhound

Bloodhound
Borzoi
Dachshund
English Foxhound
Greyhound
Harrier
Irish Wolfhound
Norwegian Elkhound
Otterhound
Rhodesian Ridgeback
Saluki
Scottish Deerhound
Whippet
Alaskan Malamute
Belgian Malinois
Belgian Sheepdog
Belgian Tervuren
Bernese Mountain Dog
Bouvier Des Flandres
Boxer
Briard
Bullmastiff
Collie
Doberman Pinscher
German Shepherd
Giant Schnauzer
Great Dane
Great Pyrenees
Komondor
Kuvasz
Mastiff
Newfoundland

Old English Sheepdog
Puli
Rottweiler
Samoyed
Shetland Sheepdog
Siberian Husky
Standard Schnauzer
St. Bernard
Welch Corgi
Airedale Terrier
Australian Terrier
Bedlington Terrier
Border Terrier
Bull Terrier
Cairn Terrier
Dandie Dinmont Terrier
Fox Terrier
Irish Terrier
Kerry Blue Terrier
Lakeland Terrier
Manchester Terrier
Miniature Schnauzer
Norwich Terrier
Scottish Terrier
Sealyham Terrier
Skye Terrier
Staffordshire Terrier
Welsh Terrier
West Highland White Terrier
Boston Terrier
Bulldog
Chow Chow

Dalmatian
French Bulldog
Keeshond
Lhasa Apso
Poodle
Schipperke
Affenpinscher
Brussels Griffon
Chihuahua
English Toy Spaniel
Italian Greyhound
Japanese Spaniel
Maltese
Manchester Terrier
Miniature Pinscher
Papillon
Pekingese
Pomeranian
Pug
Silky Terrier
Yorkshire Terrier
And all the Rest…
Admit you like dogs
You know you do
They are nice creatures
I love dogs
They are helpful
Remove depression
They make you happy
They are man's best friend
They reduce stress
They reduce blood pressure

They sit at your feet
They love unconditionally
They give kisses

My Mentor

When my body is gone,
My soul will be above;
Noah my mentor and a song.

I will tend to the dogs,
Learning from Noah my friend;
Jesus I worship you, so strong!

Pails to clean, floors to scrub,
Heaven is still a place of work;
Brushing dogs and a groomer's tub.

When my body is gone,
My soul will be above;
Noah my mentor and a song.

I will help Noah and his sons,
As a disciple I will learn;
Jesus I worship you, so strong!

Feeding dogs, trimming nails,
Heaven is still a place of work;
Drying dogs and wagging tails.

Cold Rain

The ram's horn sounded,
The weather took a twist.
Poodle dogs fearful; their hearts pounded.
The devil bangs with his fist.
Cold rain…

Cold rain, soaking dog fur,
Dampened soil, fertilizer reeks.
A multitude of lonely animals, in a blur.
A Water Dog takes a peek.
Cold rain…

The siren blew, rain came down in hailstones,
Nature on hold, Saturday gone.
Near the barn, just plows and shovels,
A Kansas downpour; Titanic song.
Cold rain…

Now waves, carrying helpless creatures,
Heads raised up, engaged in a newborn dog paddle.
Cold rain suffocates their features,
Clinging dogs, floating objects; a horse saddle.
Cold rain…

A tidal wave down Main Street,
Onlookers watch dogs swimming,
Three days strong; now soaking feet.
But it's over now, with canine grins and dogs singing.
Cold rain…

Christmas Morning

Droplets of condensation, on frosted glass,
The smell of a cooking ham.
Feels like Sunday; peace and serenity at last.

Cool snowflakes compete for landing,
So quiet, my Labrador thinks.
Outdoors, creatures scurry; nature planning.

Ornaments, light bulbs, pine tree; a carnival.
Shiny boxes, and gifts.
Inside so warm; holiday twinkle.

Down the street, powdery snow piles,
Hot tea and biscuits, cry out…
To lonely icicles so quiet.

Indoors, pine needles give flavor;
Stockings, hanging over the fireplace.
Labrador covered by a blanket, lazy.

Incredible feeling of love, and warmth,
As puppies breathe near sugar cookies,
At my feet, Labrador swarms.

Awaken

When I awaken, I shall see the Holy one,
A tabernacle permanent and precious stones,
I hear the barking dogs outside;
The twelve patriarchs, Noah and the Son.

When I awaken, I shall be engulfed in dogs warm;
Comfort, security, blessings and love.
Healing of the nations, truth swarms.
A multitude of kennel dogs, they push-and-shove.

When I awaken, I shall taste the Water of Life,
Mountains so high, Jasper and crystal.
A city wall with Twelve Foundations, pure gold and Jesus
Christ.
Sapphire, emeralds, topaz and beryl.

When I awaken, my Labrador I shall embrace,
Beagles, Hounds, Schnauzers and Golden Doodles;
Only to know the love of God's grace,
Sheepdogs, Collies, Daschunds and Poodles.

Altar Call

Up the mountainside, near the quarry,
Men left a deserted altar;
Building nests, confident swallows and sparrows.

A Golden Retriever with Heaven in his eyes,
Barks vascularly, trembling in Pentecost.
Bowing humbly, the dog looks up to the sky.

Gathering up the pack, the Retriever grins,
Dogs wearing white garments seeking confession;
Sunday there will be an altar call, the erasing of sins.

Tough street dogs, with wicked histories,
Shed their skins, disgusted with their behavior.
Parading, up to the deserted altar, eagerly.

A multitude of dogs, bowing low,
Seeking removal of predatory precociousness,
Asking for second chances; for clean souls.

Goldfish

On the counter, sits a goldfish,
In a small globular container.
He only wants one silly wish.

The Great Dane, gives him the eye.
Sourly, licks at the clear water,
A solitary fish with tears in his eyes.

On the counter, sits a goldfish,
In a small globular container,
He only wants one silly wish.

The goldfish was granted his wish!
The Great Dane gave him the eye;
Swimming to the surface; the dog kisses the fish.

Dog Days

Curious
Humor
Round worms
Cages
Leaking
Raincoat
Snapper
Quarantine
Hugs
Kisses
Agony
Whelp
Biscuits
Gravy
Ecstasy
Puppies
Vitreous humor
X-Ray
Children
Barking
Dog house
Rain
Sun
Kennel club
Dog shows
Groomer
Housebreaking
Obedience school
Ribbon

Chained In

Junk yard dogs, ferocious, unmerciful,
Poking at chunks of meat.
Chained in, dangerous, a handful.

Ravenous dogs, tan in color, with square jaws;
Tough-looking, muscular, overwhelmingly powerful.

Junk yard dogs, frayed coats, ragged,
The perfume of a chicken carcass.
Chained in, day-to-day, curmudgeon.

Ravenous dogs, tan in color, with square jaws;
Tough-looking, muscular, overwhelmingly powerful.

Junk yard dogs, parading like roosters,
The perfume of a dog penitentiary.
Chained in, pantomine; depressing colors.

Ravenous dogs, tan in color, with square jaws;
Tough-looking, muscular, overwhelmingly powerful.

Lonely

Little Brussels Griffon,
Peasant dog; animated personality;
"Please don't leave me alone."

Little Brussels Griffon,
Abandonment; nobody ever home,
Smelly shoes, searching for bones.

Little Brussels Griffon,
Who says you are ugly?
No touch, no talk, dysfunction.

Little Brussels Griffon,
Your wiry coat is mildew,
Cruel dog owner neglects you.

Little Brussels Griffon,
So shy, timid, alive.
Your real friends, are in slumberous Heaven.

Hot Day

Camel spoor, footprints,
Pausing for bitter herbs;
The desert always intimidates.

Stationary palms, fanning,
Waiting for cool temps;
Too hot, with birds landing.

Dehydrated onions,
Run from their skins;
Wilderness dry, with sun.

Dogs stay inside now,
Slumbering on cool stones,
Somebody left a winepress, a trough.

Lazy Cats

Look at the lazy cats!
Striped cats, polka-dot cats,
Calico cats, tabby cats,
Yawning cats.

Too tired to play in yarn, cats.
Chasing each other in the barn, cats.

Look at the lazy cats!
Short-haired cats, long-haired cats,
Horizontal cats and vertical cats,
Yawning cats.

Too tired to clean their room, cats.
Licking honey from spoon, cats.

Look at the lazy cats!
Orange cats, white cats,
Black and blue cats,
Yawning cats.

Patmos

Gatekeepers and doorkeepers,
Guarding walled cities, or temples;
The Romans hid their exiles.

Guard dogs, Mastiffs, tough love;
Standing at the Island Patmos,
Powerful dogs, muscular and rough.

A prison for gospel people,
"Innocent," "Innocent," they shout.
Only wanted to build church steeples.

So the big dogs keep them in,
Near the Aegean Sea,
A place where John had visions.

Mastiffs, large powerful dogs inside,
Persecution of honest souls,
With these dogs, no place to hide.

Dog Argument

…So the dogs had it their way?
But now they argued over fast foods;
Which restaurant and time-of-day.

"I want a Whopper," declared Rufus,
"No, I want a Big Mac," insisted Maggie Mae,
"Give me a small fries," said Brutus.

…So the dogs got it their way,
And now they did whatever they wanted;
Activities, fun, tug-o-war, games to play.

"I want breadsticks from Pizza Hut,"
"I want Kentucky Fried Chicken,"
Each dog voiced their demand, in a New York minute.

…So the dogs got it their way,
Up in Heaven, they have a lot of fun,
Activities, fun, tug-o-war, games to play.

Dog Rainbow

"No more floods", God said,
Noah's hands were full.
The birds, cattle and all the beasts, shall lie down.

The water will not rise again!
Now dogs of all breeds,
Looked up to the warm Son.

A magnificent rainbow in the clouds,
Adopted American and English Foxhounds.
Nice hunting dogs sitting on rainbows.

"No more floods," God said,
The shepherds gathered their flocks,
Farming, outdoor work, and sheep again.

A wonderful rainbow in the clouds,
Adopted Irish Wolfhounds and Scottish Deerhounds.
Intelligent dog breeds, just sitting around.

White Castle

Hungry dogs, sitting on stools,
Hungry dogs seeking meat.
Rottweilers and Poodles in booths.

"Those taste good," said Rufus the Rottweiler,
Gulping down the old-fashioned sliders.
A Pit Bull ate his burgers in total excitement.

Topped off by a Coca Cola, a tasty meal!
Dogs from Jerusalem streets, happy now,
French fries, burgers and wagging tails.

A family of Welsh Corgis laughed,
Cardigan and Pembroke dogs;
After lunch, time for dog baths.

So they swallow their tasty hamburgers,
With so much enthusiasm in a burger joint,
"I want a milkshake," yelled an Airedale Terrier.

Silly Cats

Silly cats,
Purring.

Silly cats,
Stirring.

Silly cats,
On their towers.

Silly cats
Hide from rain showers.

Today

Now
Now
Now
Now
Now
Now
Now
Now
Now
Now
Now
Now
Now
Now
Now
Now
Now
Live
Now

Dog House

A little dog house is empty,
Outside in the back.
It kept her dry; Rusty.

Her paws dragged mud in.
She smiled often, like a child.
Your heart she would win.

Her tail wagged excitedly,
A highlight was suppertime;
A kiss on your chin unexpectedly.

A little dog house is empty,
Outside in the back.
It kept her dry; Rusty.

Dog Soul

Please don't tell me, "It's just a dog."
I know they have a soul;
Windows of Heaven open, to a new song.
Leashes, collars and food bowls.

Please don't tell me, "You're all wrong."
I know they have a soul;
A blessing of the animals, St. Francis,
A church building is where they go.

The Patron Saint of Animals,
Is remembered every October.
Even a monk leads the elephants,
Through port holes of glory, forever.

Please tell me, "They have a soul,"
Canticle of the Creatures,
An ode to God's living things…
Opens the door to Heaven's features.

Thanksgiving

Turkey
Ham
Stuffing
Gravy

Grandma
Apple pie
Pumpkin pie
American flag

Labrador
Parade
Laughing
Children

Wet puddles
Snowflakes
Football
Autumn leaves

Shopping mall
Anticipation
Visitors
Hugs

Tough Guy

One thing; a Pit Bull will never be defeated,
This tough guy was made to fight, to the end.
In the wrong hands can lead to tragedy,
But sometimes he makes the heart bend.

Roaming near garbage cans, with snake eyes,
Only certain people can handle them.
As puppies, tender-to-the-touch, honest eyes;
As adults, can make a person helpless.

One thing; a Pit Bull will never back down,
This tough guy was made to fight, to the end.
In the wrong hands can lead to tragedy,
But sometimes he makes the heart bend.

Coming out of alleys, from evil places,
Only certain individuals beat them.
As puppies, abused and tortured to fight,
A vicious circle that will never end.

One thing; a Pit Bull will never back down,
This tough guy was made to fight, to the end.
In the wrong hands can lead to tragedy,
But sometimes he makes the heart bend.

Church

Faith
Services
Bible
Pastor

Jesus
Cleansing
Communion
Holy Spirit

Water baptism
Resurrection
Eternal
Music

Worship
Altar
Gifts
Singing

Saints
Sinners
Customs
Forgiveness

Bake sale
Chocolate chip
Tin foil
Tired

Cold Stare

I once met a Rottweiler,
Was calm on the leash,
But in his eyes, I saw the fire;
A cold stare, unable to extinguish.

Now his personality was workable,
But something was just not right,
His cold stare was unstoppable,
An inner disposition, a drive to fight.

I felt uneasy, my stomach queasy,
It was like death, Armageddon;
This dog story was just not easy,
Rottweiler bringing out my nervous energy.

He was fixated on me, fixated,
Everything got quiet before the storm.
My heart was beating, low oxygenation,
Rising blood pressure, not the norm.

I once met a Rottweiler,
Was calm on the leash,
But in his eyes, I saw the fire;
A cold stare, unable to extinguish.

On my Arm

At the kennel,
I had an alligator on my arm.

At the kennel,
I had a bad day at the farm.

At the kennel,
I had a mean dog biting.

At the kennel,
I had a bad boy fighting.

At the kennel,
I really wasn't scared.

At the kennel,
I should have brought a sword.

At the kennel,
Sometimes they just snap.

At the kennel,
My arm I just wrap.

Dogs in the Bible

Exodus 11:7

'But against none of the children of Israel shall a dog move its tongue, against man or beast, that you may know that the LORD does make a difference between the Egyptians and Israel.'

Exodus 22:31

"And you shall be holy men to Me: you shall not eat meat torn by beasts in the field; you shall throw it to the dogs.

Judges 7:5

So he brought the people down to the water. And the LORD said to Gideon, "Everyone who laps from the water with his tongue, as a dog laps, you shall set apart by himself; likewise everyone who gets down on his knees to drink."

I Samuel 17:43

So the Philistine said to David, "Am I a dog, that you come to me with sticks?" And the Philistine cursed David by his gods.

I Samuel 24:14

"After whom has the King of Israel come out? Whom do you pursue? A dead dog? A flea?

2 Samuel 3:8

Then Abner became very angry at the words of Ishbosheth, and said, “Am I a dog’s head that belongs to Judah? Today I show loyalty to the house of Saul your father, friends, to his brothers, and to his friends, and have you not delivered you into the hand of David; and you charge me today with a fault concerning this woman?

2 Samuel 9:8

Then he bowed himself, and said, “What is your servant, that you should look upon such a dead dog as I?”

2 Samuel 16:9

Then Abishai the son of Zeruiah said to the king, “Why should this dead dog curse my lord the king? Please, let me go over and take off his head!”

I Kings 14:11

“The dogs shall eat whoever belongs to Jeroboam and dies in the city, and the birds of the air shall eat whoever dies in the field; for the LORD has spoken!”

I Kings 16:4

“The dogs shall eat whoever belongs to Baasha and dies in the city, and the birds of the air shall eat whoever dies in the fields,”

I Kings 21:19

"You shall speak to him, saying, 'Thus says the LORD: "Have you murdered and also taken possession?" ' And you shall speak to him, saying, 'Thus says the LORD: "In the place where dogs licked the blood of Naboth, dogs shall lick your blood, even yours." ' "

I Kings 21:23

"And concerning Jezebel the LORD also spoke, saying, 'The dogs shall eat Jezebel by the wall of Jezreel.'

I Kings 21:24

"The dogs shall eat whoever belongs to Ahab and dies in the city, and the birds of the air shall eat whoever dies in the field."

I Kings 22:38

Then someone washed the chariot at a pool in Samaria, and the dogs licked up his blood while the harlots bathed, according to the word of the LORD which He had spoken.

2 Kings 8:13

So Hazael said, "But what is your servant a dog, that he should do this gross thing?" And Elisha answered, "The LORD has shown me that you will become king over Syria."

2 Kings 9:10

‘The dogs shall eat Jezebel on the plot of ground at Jezreel, and there shall be none to bury her.’ ” And he opened the door and fled.

2 Kings 9:36

Therefore they came back and told him. And he said, “This is the word of the LORD, which He spoke by His servant Elisha the Tishbite, saying, ‘On the plot of ground at Jezreel dogs shall eat the flesh of Jezebel;

Job 18:11

Terrors frighten him on every side, and drive him to his feet.

Job 30:1

“But now they mock at me, men younger than I, whose fathers I disdained to put with the dogs of my flock.

Psalm 22:16

For the dogs have surrounded Me; The congregation of the wicked has enclosed Me. They pierced My hands and My feet.

Psalm 22:20

Deliver Me from the sword, My precious life from the power of the dog.

Psalm 59:6

At evening they return, they growl like a dog, and go all around the city.

Psalm 59:14

And at evening they return, they growl like a dog, and go all around the city.

Psalm 68:23

That your foot may crush them in blood, and the tongues of your dogs may have their portion from your enemies."

Proverbs 26:11

As a dog returns to his own vomit, so a fool repeats his folly.

Proverbs 26:17

He who passes by and meddles in a quarrel not his own is like one who takes a dog by the ears.

Ecclesiastes 9:4

But for him who is joined to all the living there is hope, for a living dog is better than a dead lion.

Isaiah 56:10

His watchmen are blind, they are all ignorant; they are all dumb dogs, they cannot bark; sleeping, lying down, loving to slumber.

Isaiah 56:11

Yes, they are greedy dogs which never have enough. And they are shepherds who cannot understand; they all look to their own way, every one for his own gain, from his own territory.

Isaiah 66:3

"He who kills a bull is as if he slays a man; he who sacrifices a lamb, as if he breaks a dog's neck: he who offers a grain offering, as if he offers swine's blood; he who burns incense, as if he blesses an idol. Just as they have chosen their own ways, and their soul delights in their abominations,

Jeremiah 15:3

"And I will appoint over them four forms of destruction," says the LORD: "The sword to slay, the dogs to drag, the birds of the heavens and the beasts of the earth to devour and destroy.

Matthew 7:6

"Do not give what is holy to the dogs; nor cast your pearls before swine, lest they trample them under their feet, and turn and tear you in pieces.

Matthew 15:26

But He answered and said, "It is not good to take the children's bread and throw it to the little dogs."

Matthew 15:27

And she said, “Yes, Lord, yet even the little dogs eat the crumbs which fall from their master’s table.”

Mark 7:27

But Jesus said to her, “Let the children be filled first, for it is not good to take the children’s bread and throw it to the little dogs.”

Mark 7:28

And she answered and said to Him, “Yes Lord, yet even the little dogs under the table eat from the children’s crumbs.”

Luke 16:21

“desiring to be fed with the crumbs which fell from the rich man’s table. Moreover the dogs came and licked his sores.

Philippians 3:2

Beware of dogs, beware of evil workers, beware of the mutilation!

2 Peter 2:22

But it has happened to them according to the true proverb: “A dog returns to his own vomit.” And, “a sow, having washed, to her wallowing in the mire.”

Revelation 22:15

But outside are dogs and sorcerers and sexually immoral and murderers and idolaters, and whoever loves and practices a lie.

Rin Tin Tin

A box office hit,
Rin Tin Tin!

After World War I,
Your heart he has won.

The Shepherd appeared in:
Where the North Begins,
The Night Cry,
And, *Jaws of Steel.*

A box office hit,
Rin Tin Tin!

From Germany,
He brought harmony.

The Shepherd appeared in:
The Frozen River,
A Dog of the Regiment,
...And so much more.

A box office hit,
Rin Tin Tin!

Gold Sparrow

I saw a painted bird,
Outside my window.
Nature's wand, created.

The gold sparrow, was,
Riding on a Labrador's shoulder,
Man's best friend.

It's amazing how they get along,
Like lovers, shyly cooperative;
Then the sparrow sung a song.

But I heard His Mighty voice,
Up in the clouds,
And Heaven is the Labrador's choice.

Both the sparrow and the dog,
Will someday meet,
Up above, on golden streets.

Dog Bone City

These city streets smell, of perfume and evil,
Nylons hang on bed posts; dirty underwear.
Babylon, a place of sin and upheaval.

Nobody ever wants to be a "harlot,"
But heathen worship and the devil sing,
To souls corrupted in Dog Bone City.

Here, you're an animal, fighting for survival,
Swords packed on broad hips; metal shiny.
If you're lucky man, grab your Bible.

Nobody ever gets out of harlot practice,
They are controlled by wicked men;
Sitting on a urine soaked mattress.

But they say God forgives ALL sin,
And in Dog Bone City,
If you repent, and put away evil…you can win.

Parasites

Flies, fleas, lice and ticks,
Be careful where the dog licks.

Round worms, stable flies, and cattle grub,
Rocky Mountain wood ticks.

Blow flies, mites and mange,
Nonchalantly mess with swine.

The Guinea pig fur mite, tropical rat mite,
Never bother dogs or bite.

However, nematodes very gross,
Tapeworms, protozoa and nematodes.

Slugs, lungworms and liver flukes,
Offer kindness, but sure to make you puke.

Coffee

Thirsty for a slow fizz,
An elephant buzzed on lime skins.
A Beagle wanted black gold,
Sobriety and straight he sold.

The elephant was high on peach pits,
He danced like a Bulldog, then he spit.
The Beagle competed for coffee grains,
The elephant trumpeted like a hurricane.

Both animals fought a donkey,
Both animals were high and funky.
Coffee isn't really gold you know,
The elephant danced, he stole the show.

Moonlight Jo Jo

I was walking Jo Jo all alone,
Through a dark forest;
He works so hard to earn a bone.

Just him, myself and God,
With the moonlight shining off his back.
Together, a partner; two peas in a pod.

I witnessed his sensitivity,
Sweet blinking eyes;
I rubbed his neck so gently.

He revealed a soft side,
One I had never seen before.
He was my protector, in the dark of night.

Moonlight Jo Jo (a Bulldog), so powerful,
Had a life of abuse,
Traumatized, shaken, but a puppy still.

Someday Jo Jo will board the dog ladder,
Climbing up to Heaven's gates;
His presence there, surely will matter.

Volcano Dogs

The sky turned an amethyst blue,
Burning hail pellets marked the earth.
Rufus the Rottweiler was out picking myrrh;
Not really worried, collecting bitter herbs.

Out of nowhere, the volcano erupted,
Mount Jeremiah had its own agenda.
Rufus collected the young dogs,
A cloud of sulphur gas corrupted.

On Straight Street everyone was calm,
Dogs carrying umbrellas; putrid suffocate.
Rufus got the pack under broken shingles,
Earthworms competed for lemon balm.

Nobody got injured though,
Burning hail pellets… melted snow.
Volcano dogs, volcano dogs,
On a mountain side, there they go.

Marriage Dogs

So the Belgian Sheepdog agreed,
Asking the pastor for a wedding;
To *"Chien de Berger,"* a farmer's dog.
Oh Belgian Sheepdog take your wife,
Do not shy away, and be the leader.
"Chien" agreed, a contract for life.

Now madly in love, the dogs eloped,
Finding a warm nest off the road.
Their hearts ticking, a lust embargo.
The Belgian Sheepdog announced,
"I will wait till the wedding night,"
And *"Chien de Berger"* also agreed.

The pastor found the couple engaged,
Twisting…
Dancing…
Loving…
In an incredible love rage;
Just married.

Fat Cats

Wow! Fat cats
Big meaty cats
Fat cats, obese cats

Hungry, fish-eating cats
Salivating cats
Lick-the-bowl cats

Heavy cats
Wow! Fat cats
Weigh-a-ton cats

Tabby cats
Calico cats
Albino cats

Hungry, sardine-eating cats
Tuna fish cats
Salmon cats

Wow! Fat cats
Big meaty cats
Fat cats, obese cats

Sick Cats

The cattery was a place of depression,
Non-profit low; an economic recession.

Nobody washed their hands,
Passing sickness—voodoo land.

Cats disoriented, dizzy and sick,
Feverish, ringworm and especially ticks.

Green exudate, in a kitten's eyes.
Mites carrying bacteria, and kennel flies.

Cutbacks on veterinary house calls,
Stomachs bulging from dirty yarn balls.

Running out of medication,
Several died; mummification.

Some workers were fired,
And new people hired.

Get the place back on track,
On the way to healthy cats!

Buck the Pit Bull

A sweet dog named Buck,
Danced in the yard,
His life, a game of luck;
Everyone loves him, a shining star.

Tug-o-war rope in his mouth,
Approaching… to play happy games.
"Good with children," they scream and shout.
Buck has earned love and fame.

Pig-skin white with eyes of loyalty,
Muscular, cheerful and innocent.
Proven to be most trustworthy,
His tender years very well spent.

Never causes a fuss or scuffle,
The size of a horse,
Without a muzzle.
Dances a rear-end "gyrate shuffle"!

This is what a Pit Bull should be,
Tender, sweet for you and me.
Never causes any harm,
Society please awaken to Bucky's charm.

Wall Dogs

Nehemiah was to rebuild the wall.
Earlier, Jerusalem collapsed with an awful fall.
Large granite blocks,
Carried on the backs of muscular dogs.

Destroyed in 586 B.C.,
Time for rebuilding the city.
Wall dogs helped in every way,
Completing the project in 52 days.

Dogs also brought wood,
Altar materials and food.
Special taxes carried in sacks,
Coins in bags, on Rottweiler backs .

Dogs brought first fruits to the city,
Huffing and puffing,
Helping many.
Wall dogs, such “good boys.”

Watchman Dogs

Patrolling Jerusalem streets,
Sweating Mastiffs, rule.
Watching over the inhabitants,
Bullmastiffs protecting the city.

Keeping track of the clock,
Big meaty dogs, serious and stern.
Guarding the gates, or towers…
The whole city block.

Watchman dogs, standing in gun towers,
Peering down to observe.
Bully breeds, Mastiffs with power;
Making sure of no trouble.

Big heavy dogs with iron collars,
Jaws immense, incredible strength.
If you're honest they won't bother,
But if you are a sinner, be careful brother!

Dog Hard Times

People, lining up in soup lines,
Charcoal faces like in a mine shaft;
Newspapers with recession headlines.

Soot, smoke; remains of a paper mill closed.
Men with big mustaches, with tears in their eyes.
Adults unemployed, drive bicycles downtown.

We need a King that can help the people,
Oh, the glory when He returns.
Ministry, ministry and church steeples.

Hard times, families eating cat and dog food,
Washing their hair in dish soap.
Hard to tell, if this life is any good.

Christmas and no gifts,
The children seeking candy;
Makes a mother want to sin.

Oh, the glory when He returns,
Get rid of this hell on earth.
Want to hear the doves chirp.

Warm dogs can kill the pain,
Warm dogs can stop the rain.
Warm dogs can make you smile.

Don't let hard times get the best of you,
Surrender to a bigger boss;
God will see you through!

Noah's Farm

Up in Heaven, on a rainy day,
The animals were ready to roll.
But these funky creatures wanted to play.

The bats of Palestine sought fruit,
Socially nocturnal and meat eaters too.
A Syrian brown bear played a flute.

Sea monsters and moles get along,
Pounding on drums and electric guitars,
Even the fat elephants trumpeted a song.

Egyptian greyhounds running in circles,
Goats and gazelle baking cookies.
Unicorns and whales sipping wine vinegar.

This is no ordinary disco,
Wolves and jackals compete for candy,
White rump antelope playing in the snow.

Little mice seeking spices,
Frantic goats attend cooking school;
A camel smoking a Lucky Strike.

Twenty-four mature oxen plow the fields,
Rhesus animals drinking wine,
Everyone seemed to enjoy the time.

Two-Thousand Sober

Once upon a time, there was a demon in a man.
Living in the tombs this unclean person,
Could never be bound; iron shackles he broke often.
Out of his mind, the man cried out insane.

Jesus ministered near the caves, met the walking corpse,
Severely devil-bound, the man pleaded for mercy.
Outside the kennel, two-thousand dogs were ruled by a pale horse.
There was only one hope for all this pity.

Jesus told the demon-horse to lead out the canines,
The horse immediately repented, then opened the floodgate of paws and tails.
Most of the two-thousand dogs were drunk on wine;
It was time to let them out of their psychological prison.

Jesus cleansed the man in a New York minute,
Now the dogs were made sober.
A lighthouse in the night; Jesus made a beckon.
Two-thousand dogs made clean, forgiven of sins...addicted no longer.

A Mean Farm

Down on the farm,
Women spit tobacco juice.
Oh Rottweiler yawn,
Big dogs and bite wounds.

The kennel is rough,
Tattoos and liquor,
Dogs raised to be tough.
The lady spits there.

Men walk with a swagger,
Biker-women streetwise,
Pant legs reveal hidden daggers.
Dogs cared for gently, under sunny skies.

Thick neck Pit Bulls yawn,
Oh Rottweiler look over yonder,
Men and women display their brawn,
Dogs sold for profit ponder.

Down on the farm,
Women spit tobacco juice.
Oh Rottweiler yawn,
Big dogs and bite wounds.

Father's House

In my Father's house,
I am blessed.
Time to scream and shout!

Tables meant for kings,
Food piled high,
My heart sings.

Potato salad, chips and cream cheese,
Dogs at my feet,
Someone make a BLT.

Pain and suffering gone,
No pain or troubles,
Nothing is wrong.

In my Father's house,
I am blessed.
Time to scream and shout!

Turn to God

Each day, millions are cast into a dungeon:
Alcohol, drugs, hopelessness and despair,
Unemployment, crime, poverty and wars.

Turn to God.

Each day, millions turn to Jesus,
Confessing sin and looking for truth.
They say God is always with us.

Turn to God.

He is the Way, He is the Light,
He is Living Water and the Great Physician.
Now surrender to end your fight…

Turn to God.

Rubbish

Junkyard dogs, near rubbish,
Junkyard dogs, so selfish.

Seeking meat, glands or gizzards,
Seeking shelter from the blizzard.

Junkyard dogs, firm and muscular,
Junkyard dogs, torn coat zephyr.

Seeking friendship in broken bottles,
Seeking help from injurious wobbles.

Junkyard dogs, near rubbish,
Junkyard dogs, so selfish.

Seeking treats and buried bones,
Seeking relief from a broken home.

Junkyard dogs, mouthful of trash,
Junkyard dogs, life so brash.

Seeking shelter from the storm,
Seeking freedom, a life so torn.

Junkyard dogs, near rubbish,
Junkyard dogs, so selfish.

I Love Dogs

I love dogs
I love dogs
I love dogs
I love dogs
I love dogs
I love dogs
I love dogs
I love dogs
I love dogs
I love dogs

Car Ride

Little Rascal, a Terrier and I,
Went driving in my Buick, last Wednesday.
Like a child, looked out the window,
Smelling the autumn breeze; nature's show.

We went to the retirement community,
Little Rascal, (was happy) in this infirmary.
Kissing the elderly on the chin,
(They wanted small dogs), not Rin Tin Tin.

Little Rascal was a great new friend,
Like a child, explored the window ledge.
The elderly couple showed him around,
A Terrier, (was happy) not a barking sound.

Burger King

Max, the Lab, his heart sings,
"Had it his way," at Burger King.

He drooled to the drive-thru window,
Put on quite a show.

A double burger into his snapper,
Even ate the hamburger wrapper!

Paw Prints on the Moon

Are there paw prints on the moon?
God, we need to know.
Is Jesus coming back soon?
God, we need to know.

Something tells me, dogs are up there;
God, we need to know.
People, I'm not crazy, don't stare.
Someday "Rufus" on the moon, I know.

It's only what YOU believe,
Don't listen to all the criticism.
But so many dog lovers will be relieved,
When "Rufus" goes to Heaven, because of the tree.

Music Dogs

How Great Thou Art! Dogs jamming, getting down;
Music, the symphony of life, just ear candy.
A Sussex Spaniel playing a nebel harp, wears no frown.

Now a Whippet jammed on a ram's horn,
Rufus the Rottweiler punched out notes on a tambourine.
Music so contagious, hookworms and roundworms enjoy the rhythmical perfume.

Dogs of all breeds dancing in the moonlight,
A Japanese Chin boogied, a Jack Russell too!
An Irish Setter, carried a flashlight.

How Great Thou Art!
Dogs danced acrobatically and erotically,
They danced from the heart.

Smell of Dogs

I have the smell of dogs,
On my hands.
Fur, oily; from dog glands.

But it is not bad,
It is beautiful;
Living creatures for me and you.

They defend your property,
Detect fires and criminals,
Guide the blind, find lost children.

Each dog has its own scent.
Some mildew, some are wet,
Recent grooming; coconut.

I love the smell of dogs,
On my hands.
Fur, oily; from dog glands.

But it is not bad,
It is beautiful;
Living creatures for me and you.

Cesar Millan

He can handle the powerful breeds,
Sowing all the right seeds.

Trustworthy and full of compassion,
Pit Bulls and Rottweiler dogs, his obsession.

Teaches the public about leadership,
A Dog Psychology Center and fellowship.

He knows how to erase aggression,
Working with people, offering suggestions.

A leader of the wolf pack,
Cesar's dogs, they watch his back.

Blessing of Animals

Basset Hound made the trumpet sound,
As Noah's ark emptied out.

St. Francis of Assisi, he blesses…
Animals coming to the churches.

The Patron Saint of Animals,
So many creatures, he lost count!

Up the aisle, there they go…
Grinning and smiling, a wonderful show.

Elephants, hippos, and foxes,
Dogs, cats and jackals.

Mollusks, sponges, sheep and swine,
Reptiles, amphibians, and chameleons.

Up the aisle, there they go…
Grinning and smiling, part of the show.

The *"Blessing of Pets"* is warmly read,
Water sprinkled over animal heads.

Basset Hound made the trumpet sound,
As Noah's ark emptied out.

Kennel

The smell of young dogs
Leashes and collars
Poop bags

German Shepherds
Meaty dogs
Kennel workers

Hoses
Water
Scrubbing

Dog food
Fishy kittens
Pleasant mood

Barking
Snow day
Rain today

Summer again
Puppies smile
Man's best friend

Kevin Rottweiler

Life's ups and downs
College dropout to doctoral student
Went to church at a late age
A kennel volunteer
Enjoys animals

Wanted to be a physician
Never made it
Bible college more interesting
Took care of 50 cats
Enjoys nature

A weekend poet
Spent adulthood in college and libraries
Enjoys movies, books and music
Life's ups and downs
Enjoys animals

Not seeking fortune or fame
Simple things in life matter
Dogs, dogs, the love of warm dogs
Warm Dogs in Heaven
Enjoys animals

Dogs in the Wilderness

Moses led the people into Sinai,
Palm trees gave shade.
Egyptian Greyhounds under blue sky.
Dogs obedient, seeking prey.

Water was bitter, but Moses made it sweet,
Troops complained of hunger and thirst.
Marching to the promised-land, blisters on their feet.
Bellies so dry, like balloons wanting to burst.

Dogs were the only hope,
Acting as guards, warriors and hunters.
Vultures pick at rib cages of antelopes.
Goats, donkeys, parched and dry summers.

Dogs for companionship, dogs for companionship.
Dogs for recreation, dogs for recreation.
Dogs for variation, dogs for variation.

Plagues

Cold Nile, Blue Nile,
Your never-ending miles.
Ancient Egypt;
Floating ships.

Dogs in packs,
Rocks on their backs.
Slave labor,
King's favor.

God brought plagues against Pharaoh;
Moses trying to set the people free.
Countless hardships,
No water for parched lips.

Rivers turned to blood, frogs everywhere;
Mosquitoes, livestock epidemics, and boils there.
Hail, darkness, the first-born died,
Destruction, sadness and the people cried.

Moses had friendly dog packs,
Heavy stones upon their backs.
Working hard to build a following,
Attempting to remove the wallowing.

Moses wanted the people free,
And removed Egyptian slavery.
Eventually God took control,
Helping Moses to overthrow.

Rufus on Herbs

Rufus the Rottweiler, tail wagging,
Muscular and in control.
Rufus relaxes on herbs, he brags.

Valerian, passion flower and celery seed,
Stops though, for oriental tea.
Catnip powder, hops; relaxing from reality.

On orange peel, he yawns briefly.
Herbal gardening, a daily treat;
Fluctuating in yogurt, turnips and chicken meat.

Rufus the Rottweiler, so healthy,
Muscular and in control.
Rufus relaxes on herbs, he brags.

Coins

Mastiff and Rottweiler dogs,
Carrying bags of coins,
Around their necks.

A denarius tribute penny,
Oh, Tiberius and Augustus reign.
A few paying taxes for many.

Money-changers and hypocrisy,
Temple tax, of Rome;
Leading to ulcers and apoplexy.

Why is money so important?
"Jerusalem is holy," an inscription.
Hard times and pennies spent.

Coins feed the people,
Blood money and compensation.
Time to build more church steeples.

Mastiff and Rottweiler dogs,
Carrying bags of coins,
Around their necks.

Mustard

Mustard the Maltese
Has yellow fleas

Mustard the Maltese
Lap dog of Greece?

Mustard the Maltese
Your coat makes me sneeze

Mustard the Maltese
Eats rotting cheese

CPSIA information can be obtained at www.ICGtesting.com
262241BV00001B/20/P

9 781456 030735